Food, Food, Food!

Food, Food, Food!	2
Story: The Cat's Dinner	9
Rhyme: The Hungry Cat	20
Activities	21
Picture Dictionary	23

Written by Paul Shipton
Illustrated by Anthony Rule

I like food

Where is food from?

Vegetables are from plants.

Potatoes and carrots grow under the ground.

Cabbages grow above the ground.

Fruit is from plants and trees.

This is an apple tree.

Bananas are from banana trees.

Eggs are from chickens.

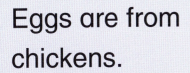

You can make an omelette with eggs.

This is a Spanish omelette.

Milk is from cows.

Cheese and yoghurt are from milk.

So cheese and yoghurt are from cows!

Meat is from animals.

chicken

burger

I like burgers with cheese and tomatoes!

Burgers are from cows.

What is your favourite food?

The Cat's Dinner

Written by Paul Shipton
Illustrated by Anthony Rule

But Max is STILL hungry.

"Mmmm. This chair is delicious!"

"A cat can't eat a chair!"

"This cat can!"

The Hungry Cat

Can I have carrots?
Can I have cheese?
Can I have an omelette?
And sausages, please?

Can I have a sandwich?
And a pizza with that?
Can I have potatoes?
I'm the hungry cat.

Can I have a banana?
And seven apples, too?
Do I like food?
OH, YES I DO!

Activities

1 Write the numbers.

This is from a tree.

This is from a cow.

This is from under the ground.

This is from a chicken.

2 Read and match.

I like cheese.

Wake up, Tiger.

I'm tired.

Who's at the door?

Picture Dictionary

Macmillan Education
4 Crinan Street,
London N1 9XW
A division of Springer Nature Limited
Companies and representatives throughout the world

ISBN 978-1-3800-4188-3

Text © Paul Shipton 2013
Design and illustration © Springer Nature Limited 2019

The author has asserted his right to be identified as the author of this work in accordance with the Copyright, Design and Patents Act 1988.

First published 2013
This edition published 2019

All rights reserved; no part of this publication may be reproduced, stored in a retrieval system, transmitted in any form, or by any means, electronic, mechanical, photocopying, recording, or otherwise, without the prior written permission of the publishers.

Designed by Carolyn Gibson
Illustrated by Anthony Rule
Cover photograph by **Alamy**/Alex Segre
Picture research by Victoria Townsley-Gaunt

The author and publishers would like to thank the following for permission to reproduce their photographs:
Alamy/Stock Connection Blue p3(b), Alamy/foodfolio p1, Alamy/Mouse in the House p7(c), Alamy/Dinodia Photos p4(r), Alamy/Trevor Ronson Photographic p4(l), Alamy/Gary K Smith p3(tl); **Corbis**/Alan Marsh/First Light p8, Corbis/Maximilian Stock Ltd/the food passionates p6(b), Corbis/Davide Erbetta/SOPA p7(b); **Getty Images**/Peter Anderson p5(t), Getty Images/EyeEm/Banu Patel p6(b), Getty Images/Kathy Collins p3(tr), Getty Images/Peter Dazeley p2; Getty Images/iStock/Anna_Om p1, **Glow Images**/Le Studio p7(t); **Plain Pictures**/Design pics p6(t); **Stockbyte** pp6(t), 7(b); **SuperStock**/Food Collection p5(b).

These materials may contain links for third party websites. We have no control over, and are not responsible for, the contents of such third party websites. Please use care when accessing them.

The inclusion of any specific companies, commercial products, trade names or otherwise does not constitute or imply its endorsement or recommendation by Springer Nature Limited.

Printed and bound in Great Britain by Bell and Bain Ltd, Glasgow

2023 2022 2021 2020 2019
10 9 8 7 6 5 4 3 2 1